JIM ALONG, JOSIE

BOOKSALE

JIM ALONG, JOSIE

A Collection of Folk Songs
and Singing Games for Young Children

Compiled by

NANCY and JOHN LANGSTAFF

Piano arrangements by Seymour Barab
Guitar chords by Happy Traum
Optional percussion accompaniments for children

Illustrated by JAN PIENKOWSKI

HARCOURT BRACE JOVANOVICH, INC.
NEW YORK

DEFGHIJ

ISBN 0-15-240250-0

Library of Congress Catalog Card Number: 79-115757

PRINTED IN THE UNITED STATES OF AMERICA

Music engraving by Irwin Rabinowitz

The title of this book is taken from the song "Jim Along, Josie" in *The American Play-Party
Song*, collected by B. A. Botkin and published by the University of Nebraska Press.

Preface

The songs we have chosen for this collection reflect our basic tenet that music for young children should be tremendous fun and of the best quality. These are songs that both the children and we have enjoyed over the years and that have remained fresh and lively for us, even after countless repetition. Many are songs that lend themselves to mime, acting out, or dancing, because small children are irresistibly drawn to moving to music. Being mostly folk tunes and having gone through many variations and changes to reach their present form, they also lend themselves to improvisation by the children, who delight in making up their own words and actions. Because children need a flexible and imaginative approach, these are songs that can be used in a variety of ways or as stepping stones to a child's own creative work.

Experienced teachers will have their own methods and, of course, will cull only what they need, so we have directed these notes toward those who are less experienced and who may be interested in some of the ways in which we have used these songs over the years.

We attempt to combine many elements in our classes: singing, free rhythms, play party games, the use of percussion instruments, beginning note learning, and improvisation. Of course, it is possible to go into any one of these in depth with a specialized teacher (such as modern dance), but we have felt the value of drawing all these elements together from the standpoint of the music itself, to make a rounded experience.

The songs and the singing are the heart of our work. The verses are often the child's first contact with poetry. The tunes, with their variety of beauty, of melodic line, or rhythmic vigor, are doorways to the finest in music; and the involvement of the child who is totally wrapped up in the singing of a song is a truly valid musical experience.

We try to have the children sing musically, with good phrasing, clear enunciation, and sensitivity to dynamics, from the very beginning. If children are encouraged to sing softly enough so that they can listen to each other, it helps to develop their sense of pitch and tonal quality. They should first hear a verse of the song to gain an impression of its tune, rhythm, and style. We often teach the refrains next, so that the children can join in and participate as the song unfolds. Many songs have repeating lines which the children can echo back, like "Cocky Robin." Others have verses that differ in only a couple of words, like "Lazy John," so that children can sing the entire song almost immediately. Of course, it is essential for the teacher to memorize the songs and singing games before class, so that he can give his full attention to the children. If playing the piano or guitar gets between you and the children and you cannot look at their faces and sing with them while playing, dispense with it and use only your voice. Don't be hesitant about unaccompanied singing. Originally, folk songs were always sung this way!

Be ready to adapt your material and approach for different ages and different concentration spans. The youngest children may need to sing a song in a slower tempo than the seven- or eight-year-olds, and may learn one verse where the others quickly learn six!

The traditional singing games that we have included, combining singing, dance movement and drama, have been enjoyed by children for centuries. How can a child be more totally involved than to make his own music through singing, while dancing and acting out the words? While immersed in the world of make-believe of these games, children respond unselfconsciously and spontaneously to their rhythms. For this reason, it is important to let young children give full vent to their imaginations in interpreting the actions and movements suggested by the song. At times, the smallest children will all want to interpret individually, and we may have a dozen "Mulberry Bushes" all at once. At other times, it is helpful for the teacher to suggest a dance framework, such as joining hands in a circle with one child in the middle, and letting the actions develop from this point. On the other hand, children in the second and third grades often welcome the challenge of learning the traditional patterns for games like "The Noble Duke of York." So there is room for a great deal of flexibility in the use of singing games, and it should be noted that our directions may be only one of several kinds that we have used or that the children have devised.

Usually, the tunes and movements of singing games stem from the rhythmic cadence of the words. "Two in the middle and you can't jump Josie" and "Here comes Sally" are close to the natural chanting of children. So we learn the songs first, usually sitting on the floor, without any accompaniment. (Since the children, through their singing, will be making their own dance music, addition of piano or other instruments can get in the way.) The singing should be musical at all times, even when the movements are added, and never degenerate into shouting. A deft touch is sometimes needed to keep the game in hand, so that there is involvement without rowdiness. However, it is wise for the teacher to efface himself as much as possible after the song has been learned and just join in the game, letting the impulse for movement and actions come from the children. A strong feeling of unity and cooperation often arises among them—after all, a circle dance is one of the first ways a tiny child connects with his group. One five-year-old, involved in playing "Old Roger," told her friends, "Don't let go your hands or the magic will be broken!"

The songs we have put under the heading of "Action Songs" are particularly suited to the youngest children. The shy child will often join in the mime of such songs and "play nicknack on my thumb" long before he feels confident enough to sing "This Old Man." These action songs leave a great deal of scope for the inventiveness of the children, and the movement can be quite individual. Some children will want to mime quietly with their hands and fingers as they sing, others to move about on the floor. Making up new verses is also part of the fun and can serve as an introduction to a child making up his own songs. One kindergarten group made up dozens of verses (with appropriate actions!) for "A-Hunting We Will Go" and were delighted with their own humor in "We'll catch a goat and put him in a boat" and the ridiculousness of "We'll catch a whale and put him in a pail"!

The use of percussion instruments, if they are handled musically, can be a rewarding experience for children. Usually, these will be the first instruments that children play, and it should be stressed that the triangles, drums, claves, etc., are real instruments, used in orchestras, and not noisemakers! Each one has its own timbre, and children, through careful listening, soon become aware of the different tone colors and relative pitches and like to suggest what instruments are appropriate for accompanying various songs. One first-grade group chose drums and claves (or rhythm sticks) for the first part of "Daddy Shot a Bear"; then kept very quiet for one child to accompany the singing of "Shot him through a keyhole" with a triangle; then finished triumphantly with all instruments on "and never touched a hair!" Children enjoy accompanying their songs, and this increases their rhythmic skill and helps to teach them about phrasing. At first they are apt to only follow the word rhythms: "Gó ańd téll Aúnt Nán-ćy." Soon they begin to feel a musical pulse and can be encouraged to use a more independent beat. Seven- and eight-year-olds can use two or more different beats simultaneously and vary them with changes in the song. Overemphasis of accent on the first beat of every bar should be avoided, and longer phrases should be emphasized. A great many of the tunes in this collection are splendid for light percussion or rhythmic clapping on the "off-beat."

We have included some optional percussion accompaniments that the children can use to accompany their singing and that may be helpful in leading to the children's own improvisation. The simple counter melody or ostinato can be played on chime bars, glockenspiel, xylophone, piano, recorder, tuned bottles or glasses, etc. For non-pitch rhythm accompaniments, we have used drums, claves, maracas, flower pots, triangles, tambourines, and pie tins. The children will have lots of ideas! However, the sound of the "instruments" chosen should be appropriate to the mood of the song.

A few words might be added concerning children's voices and their singing. It is important to have the children sit up straight. Good posture is essential for good singing! As a general rule, loud singing is to be avoided. Singing should be soft enough so that the phrases can be shaped dynamically and so that children have an awareness of tone quality and ensemble. Listening, while singing, also helps the child with an insecure sense of pitch to match his tones with others. Children like the challenge of figuring out where to breathe so that they can sing through the longer phrases, and of working out simple dynamics. Children are never too young to have a feeling for a melodic line, or the rise and fall of words. The natural tendency of the human voice should be to rise in volume and intensity as the musical phrase ascends, and to lessen as a phrase descends and diminishes. An easy way to have children "see" this is to contour the rising and falling musical lines with your hand in the air. The ocean wave that builds up and up, then falls away again, illustrates this principle.

Sloppy enunciation is another area in which the teacher can help. Have the children open their mouths enough when they sing vowels, and make use of their tongue and lips to articulate the words. They will soon find that clear enunciation actually helps to brighten and place the tone, and may even influence accuracy of pitch. (A number of songs in this book have refrains of nonsense syllables that are amusing for exercising rhythmic enunciation.) All these suggestions can be introduced with a light touch, because children catch on incredibly quickly and are stimulated by the development of these singing skills.

Above all, music should be fun. Let your own enthusiasm communicate itself to the children as you make music together!

Nancy and John Langstaff

Using the Guitar

The guitar chords provided with the music in this collection have been arranged with the novice in mind. They have been simplified as much as possible, and where the chords are unavoidably difficult, alternates have been given. Many of the songs here can even be played by a beginning guitar student who may be among the class-room children. (In fact, this book will make an excellent songbook for a guitar teacher with beginning children's groups.) The chords, of course, may be used for other instruments as well, e.g., banjo, ukulele, concertina, autoharp, etc.

The guitar chords and the piano arrangements should be considered as two different things and often will differ to the extent that they cannot be played together. But they serve two very different functions. The piano arrangement is a composed setting and will be played, for the most part, as written. You, the guitarist, will have only the chords to go by, and your accompaniment can be as simple or as complex as you wish, depending on what skills you have at your command.

As with any instrument, certain keys present more of a problem to the novice than others. If you are a beginner, you will prefer those keys that enable you to play with a minimum of barred chords and long stretches. A, C, D, E, and G are the easiest keys on the guitar. In those places in which the more difficult chords are used (Bb, for instance), I have chorded the song two ways: the actual chord used and (in parenthesis) an alternate chord to be used with a *capo*. This is a clamp, sometimes metal, sometimes elastic, with a bar that presses down on all six strings simultaneously, thereby raising the pitch of the entire guitar. In this way, you can play the song in a familiar fingering but in a transposed key. Many of the songs in this book have been written in the key of F. In these cases, I have made a note to capo the third fret (Capo III) and play the chords in parentheses, which are in the easier key of D. (For example, see "Two in a Boat" on page 92, and "Frog Went A-Courtin'" on page 64.) Other songs, which may be in other "difficult" keys, are provided with similar capo instructions and alternate chords. Of course, any guitarist with some experience will be able to play any of the songs in this book without difficulty. One more thing about the capo: once you are familiar with the tune, and provided you are not playing with another instrument, you can play the alternate chords without the capo, or with the capo at *any* fret, depending on your own vocal range. Don't be afraid to experiment.

When working with children, the most important thing is that you enjoy yourself. This is immediately communicated, and the singing and creativity of both you and the children will be much enhanced. For this reason, the simpler your guitar playing is, the better the children will respond. Don't worry about fancy chords or intricate strums. Play a simple, strong rhythm and let the song take over.

Happy Traum

Contents

FOLK SONGS   13

Good-bye, Old Paint   14

Johnny, Get Your Hair Cut   15

The Keel Row   16

Hop Up, My Ladies   18

This Little Light o' Mine   20

Shanghai Chicken   21

Oh, Dear! What Can the Matter Be?   22

Who Built the Ark?   24

All the Ducks   25

If All the World Were Paper   26

The Muffin Man   27

Brother Rabbit   28

To People Who Have Gardens   30

God, Our Loving Father   31

Cocky Robin   32

Bobby Shaftoe   34

Ally Bally   35

The Little Black Bull (Hoosen Johnny)   36

Lazy John   38

Polly, Put the Kettle On   40

I Had a Little Nut Tree   41

Billy Boy   42

By'n Bye   44

The Jackfish   45

The Riddle Song (I Gave My Love a Cherry)   46

Young Lambs to Sell   48

The Tottenham Toad   49

Cock-a-Doodle-Doo   50

The Mockingbird (Hush Up, Baby)   52

Daddy Shot a Bear   53

The Allee-Allee O   54

The Little Pig   56

Phoebe in Her Petticoat   57

Lavender's Blue   58

Mary Wore a Red Dress   60

Go and Tell Aunt Nancy (Old Gray Goose)   61

Will You Wear Red?   62

Frog Went A-Courtin'   64

Willie Foster   67

SINGING GAMES   69

There Stands a Lady on a Mountain   70

Old Bald Eagle   72

Sally Go Round the Moon   73

When I Was a Young Girl (or Boy)   74

Sandy Land   75

Oats and Beans   76

Draw a Bucket of Water   78

Our Gallant Ship (Three Times Around)   79

Green Gravel   80

Jolly Is the Miller Boy   82

Here Come Two Dukes A-Riding   84

Old Roger   86

Here Comes Sally!   87

The Roman Soldiers   88

The Noble Duke of York   90

Two in a Boat   92

Bow Down, O Belinda   93

Floating Down the River (Jump Josie)   94

Captain Jinks   96

Going to Boston   98

ACTION SONGS   101

Here We Come on Our Ponies   102

The Big Procession   103

This Old Man   104

Hot Cross Buns   105

Pick a Bale of Cotton   106

See How I'm Jumping   107

Jim Along, Josie   108

Polly Perkin   109

Hush-a-bye, Baby   110

Creep, Mouse, Creep   111

John Brown Had a Little Indian   112

Punchinello   113

Sing a Song of Sixpence   114

Pop! Goes the Weasel   115

The North Wind Doth Blow   116

Hickory, Dickory, Dock   117

A-Hunting We Will Go   118

Jeremiah, Blow the Fire   119

Little Betty Martin   120

London Hill   122

Santy Maloney   123

See-saw, Sacra-down   124

INDEX OF TITLES   127

Folk Songs

GOOD-BYE, OLD PAINT

2. Oh, hitch up your horses and feed 'em some hay,
And seat yourself by me as long as you'll stay.
CHORUS

3. My horses ain't hungry, they'll not eat your h
My wagon is loaded and rolling away.
CHORUS

Cowboys sitting around a campfire sing this in a slow and lonesome way.

Note: Halves of coconut shells struck together make a fine sound of horses' hoofs.

❋ Capo III

JOHNNY, GET YOUR HAIR CUT

Crisply (♩ = 132)

Pennsylvania

John - ny, get your hair cut, hair cut, hair cut,

John - ny, get your hair cut just like me.

Ostinato: tuned instrument

Ostinato: percussion

Chime bars

Children like to sing their own names and to make up other verses: "Peter has a snowsuit," "Sally has a kitten."

From *Hill Country Tunes,* American Folklore Society, Vol. 39. Used by permission.

THE KEEL ROW

With a snappy accent (♩ = 120)

Northumberland

As I came through Sand-gate, through Sand-gate, through Sand-gate, as I came through Sand-gate, I heard a las-sie sing: "Oh, weel_may the keel row, the keel row, the keel_row, weel_may the keel row that my_ lad-die's in."

✹ Capo III

2. He wears a blue bonnet, blue bonnet, blue bonnet,
   He wears a blue bonnet,
   A dimple in his chin.
   Oh, weel may the keel row, etc.

This song is marvelous for jigging or hopping. One group can sing, making the "mouth music," while a second moves.

The tune can also be used for the Danish game "Seven Jumps":

The children spread out around the room and jig in place to the first eight measures. They stop abruptly, then say "up—down" slowly, meanwhile lifting the right knee high in the air on "up," then letting it down on "down." Then jig in place again to the song; stop; lift the right knee "up—down" again, then the left knee "up—down." The actions accumulate, added one at a time (always with the jigging in between):

Down on right knee;
Down on both knees;
Right elbow touches the ground;
Left elbow touches the ground;
Head touches the ground!

HOP UP, MY LADIES

Virginia

Dance-like (♩ = 76)

Did you ev-er go to meet-ing, Un-cle Joe, Un-cle Joe? Did you ev-er go to meet-ing Un-cle Joe?__ Did you ev-er go to meet-ing Un-cle Joe, Un-cle Joe? Don't mind the weath-er, so the wind don't blow.

Refrain

Hop up, my la-dies, three in a row, Hop up, my la-dies, three in a row,

Collected by John A. Lomax and Alan Lomax.
TRO © Copyright 1941 and renewed 1969 Ludlow Music, Inc., New York, N.Y. Used by permission.

Hop up, my la - dies, three in a row, Don't mind the weath-er, so the wind don't blow.

Ostinato: percussion

Chime bars

Refrain

2. Will your horse carry double, Uncle Joe, Uncle Joe?
     Will your horse carry double, Uncle Joe?
   Will your horse carry double, Uncle Joe, Uncle Joe?
     Don't mind the weather, so the wind don't blow.
   REFRAIN

3. Is your horse a single-footer, Uncle Joe, Uncle Joe?, *etc.*
   REFRAIN

4. Say, don't you want to gallop, Uncle Joe, Uncle Joe?, *etc.*
   REFRAIN

5. Say, you might take a tumble, Uncle Joe, Uncle Joe, *etc.*
   REFRAIN

The second section can be used by itself as an action game, varying the number of "ladies" who "hop up." Children enjoy the challenge of the syncopation of the refrain.

THIS LITTLE LIGHT O' MINE

Gently (♩=66)

Negro tradition

This lit-tle light o' mine, __ I'm goin' to let it shine.

This lit-tle light o' mine, __ I'm goin' to let it shine. This lit-tle light o'

mine, __ I'm goin' to let it shine, let it shine, let it shine, let it shine.

Ostinato: tuned instrument

Ostinato: percussion

Chime bars

2. Ev'rywhere I go,
   I'm goin' to let it shine, *etc.*

3. All through the night,
   I'm gonna let it shine, *etc.*

It is easy for children to add verses to any song with repeated lines such as this.

SHANGHAI CHICKEN

Enthusiastically (♩ = 92)

American

2. Great big fish they call a whale;   I have a home over yonder;
   Few days, few days;   Few days, few days;
   Swallowed Jonah head and tail,   I have a home over yonder,
   And I'm goin' home.   And I'm goin' home.

OH, DEAR! WHAT CAN THE MATTER BE?

With a good swing (♩. = 76)

English tradition

Oh, dear! What can the matter be? Oh, dear! What can the mat-ter be? Oh, dear! What can the mat-ter be? John-ny's so long at the fair.

He prom-ised to buy me a bunch of blue rib-bons, he

Da Capo al Fine

Ostinato: tuned instrument

Ostinato: percussion

Chime bars

After singing this through a couple of times, it's a splendid tune to jig or skip to.

WHO BUILT THE ARK?

Negro Jubilee Spiritual

2. He built it long, both wide and tall,
   Plenty of room for the big and the small.
   CHORUS

3. He found him an ax and a hammer too,
   He began to cut and began to hew.
   CHORUS

4. And every time that hammer ring,
   Old Noah shout and Noah sing.
   CHORUS

5. Now in come the animals two by two,
   Hippopotamus and kangaroo.
   CHORUS

6. Now in come the animals three by three,
   Two big cats and a bumblebee.
   CHORUS

7. Now in come the animals four by four,
   Two through the window and two through the door.
   CHORUS

It is fun to sing the chorus responses back and forth, first with the teacher leading off, then before long with two groups of children.

From *Rolling Along in Song* edited by J. Rosamond Johnson. Copyright 1937 by The Viking Press, Inc., copyright © renewed 1965 by Mrs. Nora E. Johnson. Reprinted by permission of The Viking Press, Inc.

ALL THE DUCKS

The Netherlands

Precisely (♩ = 116)

All the ducks are swim-ming in the wa-ter, fol-de-rol-de-rol-do, fol-de-rol-de-rol-do, all the ducks are swim-ming in the wa-ter, fol-de-rol-de-rol-de-ray.

Ostinato: voice

Quack quack

Ostinato: percussion

Chime bars

✻ Capo III

The bridge is broken, however shall we mend it?
  Fol-de-rol-de-rol-do, fol-de-rol-de-rol-do,
The bridge is broken, however shall we mend it?
  Fol-de-rol-de-rol-de-ray.

3. In my boat I'll quickly row you over,
  Fol-de-rol-de-rol-do, fol-de-rol-de-rol-do,
In my boat I'll quickly row you over,
  Fol-de-rol-de-rol-de-ray.

4. Three new pennies we will gladly pay you,
  Fol-de-rol-de-rol-do, fol-de-rol-de-rol-do,
Three new pennies we will gladly pay you,
  Fol-de-rol-de-rol-de-ray.

IF ALL THE WORLD WERE PAPER

English country dance tune

Lightly (♩. = 120)

F   C

If all the world were pa - per and

F

all the seas were ink___ and all the trees were bread and cheese, what

G   1. C   *Final ending* C

would we have to drink? drink? INK!
(Shout)

Ostinato: percussion

Chime bars

It makes for suspense to sing this dance tune over twice, with no pause, before adding the final "INK"!

THE MUFFIN MAN

Lively (♩=88)

English tradition

Do you know the muf-fin man, the muf-fin man, the muf-fin man?
Do you know the muf-fin man who lives in Dru-ry Lane?

Ostinato: tuned instrument

Ostinato: percussion

Chime bars

2. Yes, I know the muffin man, the muffin man, the
   muffin man,
   Yes, I know the muffin man who lives in Drury Lane.

A charming song for the youngest children, who like to substitute their own names:
"Do you know Belinda Jones who lives on Maple Street?"

BROTHER RABBIT

With a driving rhythm (♩ = 76)

Mississippi

Knock a - long, Broth-er Rab-bit, knock a - long; knock a -
long, Broth-er Rab-bit, knock a - long; knock a - long, Broth-er Rab-bit, knock a -
long, Broth-er Rab-bit, knock a - long, Broth-er Rab-bit, knock a - long.

Met Broth-er Rab-bit in a snow-white field 'bout a mile and a half from

✻ Capo I

Transcribed from a field recording in the Archive of Folk Song, Library of Congress.

town.   I asked him where was   he goin',   says: "Goin' down to

E♭(D)   F(E)   B♭(A)

new ground   to   get that grub-bin' hoe.   Two big hounds were

Da Capo al Fine

on my track, tryin' to make it through the thick-et 'fore the sun goes down."

Ostinato: percussion   **Alternate percussion**

TO PEOPLE WHO HAVE GARDENS

Gaily (♩ = 100)

The Hebrides Islands

For day's work and week's work as I go
up and down, there are man-y gar-dens all a-bout the town. *Fine*
One that's gay with daf-fo-dils, one where chil-dren play,____
one, white with cher-ry flow'r, the oth-er red with may. *Da Capo al Fine*

Ostinato: percussion

Chime bars

Words by Agnes More MacKenzie of Stornaway. Music arranged by Marjory Kennedy Fraser. Copyright 1921 by Boosey & Co., Ltd., Renewed 1948. Reprinted by permission of Boosey & Hawkes, Inc.

30

GOD, OUR LOVING FATHER

Sustained (♩=104)

Finnish folk tune

Who made o-cean, earth and sky? God, our lov-ing Fa - ther.

Who made sun and moon on high? God, our lov-ing Fa - ther.

Who made all the birds that fly? God, our lov-ing Fa - ther.

Ostinato: tuned instrument

Chime bars

Ostinato: percussion

✻Capo III

2. Who made lakes and rivers blue?
   God, our loving Father.
   Who made snow and rain and dew?
   God, our loving Father.
   He made little children, too,
   God, our loving Father.

Even the youngest children can join in the repeated refrain immediately.

From *140 Folk Songs*, Concord Series #7, © E. C. Schirmer Music Company, Boston, Mass. Used by permission.

COCKY ROBIN

Gaily (♩ = 168)

Kentucky

Who killed Cock-y Ro-bin? Who killed Cock-y Ro-bin? "I," said the Spar-row, "with my lit-tle bow and ar-row, it was I, it was I."

Ostinato: tuned instrument

Chime bars

Ostinato: percussion

2. Who saw him die?
   Who saw him die?
   "I," said the Fly,
   "With my little teensy eye,
   It was I, it was I."

3. Who caught his blood?, *etc.*
   "I," said the Fish,
   "With my little silver dish," *etc.*

4. Who made his coffin?, *etc.*
   "I," said the Snipe,
   "With my little pocketknife," *etc.*

5. Who dug his grave?, *etc.*
   "I," said the Crow,
   With my little spade and hoe," *etc.*

6. Who hauled him to it?, *etc.*
   "I," said the Lark,
   "With my little horse and cart," *etc.*

7. Who let him down?, *etc.*
   "I," said the Crane,
   "With my little golden chain," *etc.*

8. Who pat his grave?, *etc.*
   "I," said the Duck,
   "With my big old splatter foot," *etc.*

9. Who preached his funeral?, *etc.*
   "I," said the Swallow,
   "Just as loud as I could holler!," *etc.*

Collected by Cecil Sharp, used by permission of Novello
& Co., Ltd., London.

The tune of this charming variant is nothing more than the ancient melody pattern chanted by children in many countries: the "calling" or "chanting" interval of the descending minor third. The form of this song lends itself easily to lining-out the first and last line of each verse for the children to repeat.

BOBBY SHAFTOE

Neatly (♩ = 104)

Scottish tradition

CHORUS

2. Bobby Shaftoe's tall and slim,
   He's always dressed so neat and trim,

   The lassies they all keek at him,
   Bonny Bobby Shaftoe.

   CHORUS

ALLY BALLY

Gently ($\dot = 58$)

Al - ly bal - ly, al - ly bal - ly bee, sit - tin' on your dad - dy's knee, greet - in' for a wee pen - ny to buy some Coul - ter's can - dy.

Chime bars

Ostinato: percussion

2. Poor, wee thing you're gettin' very thin,
   A bundle of bones covered over with skin;
   Now you're gettin' a wee double chin
   From sucking Coulter's candy.

3. Go to sleep now, my little man,
   Seven o'clock and your playin's done.
   Open your eyes to the morning sun,
   And I'll give you some Coulter's candy.

Some say that there really was a Mr. Coulter who sold penny candy somewhere in Scotland. ("Greetin'" means "crying.")

THE LITTLE BLACK BULL
(HOOSEN JOHNNY)

Steadily (♩ = 76)

Illinois

The lit-tle black bull came down the mea-dow,

Hoo-sen John-ny, Hoo-sen John-ny, the lit-tle black bull came

down the mea-dow long time a-go,

long time a-go, long time a-go, the

❀ Capo III

From *The American Songbag* by Carl Sandburg, Harcourt Brace Jovanovich, Inc.

C7(A7)   F(D)

lit-tle black bull came down the mea-dow long time a - go.

Ostinato: percussion

Chime bars

2. Oh, first he paw and then he bellow,
   Hoosen Johnny, Hoosen Johnny,
   Oh, first he paw and then he bellow,
   Long time ago.
   Long time ago,
   Long time ago,
   Oh, first he paw and then he bellow,
   Long time ago.

3. He whet his horn on a white oak sapling, *etc.*

4. He shake his tail, he jar the meadow, *etc.*

5. He paw the dirt in the heifers' faces, *etc.*

LAZY JOHN

Saucily (♩=104)

North Carolina

GIRLS:

F(D)*

La-zy John, La-zy John, will you mar-ry me? Will you mar-ry me?

BOYS:

C7(A7)

1. How can I mar-ry you? No hat to wear.
2. How can I mar-ry you? No coat to wear.
3. How can I mar-ry you? No shirt to wear.
4. How can I mar-ry you? No pants to wear.
5. How can I mar-ry you? No shoes to wear.
6. How can I mar-ry you? No socks to wear.

ALL:

F(D)

C7(A7)

Up she jumped and a - way she ran down to the mar-ket square.

✿Capo III   From *The Handy Play Party Book*, © 1940 Lynn Rohrbough, Cooperative Recreation Service, Inc., Delaware, Ohio. Used by permission.

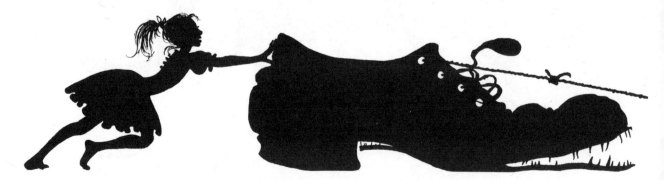

F(D)

There she found a hat for La - zy John to wear.
There she found a coat for La - zy John to wear.
There she found a shirt for La - zy John to wear.
There she found some pants for La - zy John to wear.
There she found some shoes for La - zy John to wear.
There she found some socks for La - zy John to wear.

GIRLS: F(D)

7. La-zy John, La-zy John, will you mar-ry me? Will you mar-ry me?

BOYS:

C7(A7) F(D)

How can I mar - ry you with a wife and ba- by at home?

Ostinato: tuned instrument

Ostinato: percussion

Chime bars

This can be acted out very humorously with costume props. Boys and girls like to toss these question and answer verses back and forth, adding verses of their own.

POLLY, PUT THE KETTLE ON

Gaily (♩ = 108)

English tradition

Pol - ly, put the ket-tle on, Pol-ly, put the ket-tle on,

Pol - ly, put the ket - tle on, we'll all have tea.

Su - key, take it off a - gain, Su - key, take it off a - gain,

Su - key, take it off a - gain, they've all gone a - way.

Ostinato: tuned instrument

Chime bars

Ostinato: percussion

I HAD A LITTLE NUT TREE

Lyrically (♩=96)

English tradition

I had a lit-tle nut tree, noth-ing would it bear but a sil-ver nut-meg and a gold-en pear. The King of Spain's daugh-ter came to vis-it me, and all___ for the sake of my lit-tle nut tree.

Ostinato: tuned instrument

Ostinato: percussion

Chime bars

2. Her dress was all of crimson,
   Coal black was her hair;
   She asked me for my nutmeg
   And my golden pear.

I said, "So fair a princess
Never did I see,
I'll give to you the fruit
Of my little nut tree."

BILLY BOY

Briskly ($\quarternote = 112$)

Maryland

Oh,__ where have you been, Bil - ly Boy, Bil - ly Boy? Oh,__ where have you been, charm-ing Bil-ly? I have been to seek a wife, she's the joy__ of my life, she's a young thing and can-not leave her moth-er.

Ostinato: tuned instrument

Chime bars

Ostinato: percussion

42

2. Did she bid you to come in,
   Billy Boy, Billy Boy?
   Did she bid you to come in,
   Charming Billy?
   Yes, she bade me to come in,
   There's a dimple on her chin.
   She's a young thing
   And cannot leave her mother.

3. Did she take your hat?, *etc.*
   Yes, she took my hat,
   But she threw it at the cat, *etc.*

4. Did she set for you a chair?, *etc.*
   Yes, she set for me a chair,
   But the bottom wasn't there, *etc.*

5. Can she bake a cherry pie?, *etc.*
   She can bake a cherry pie,
   Quick as cat can wink her eye, *etc.*

6. Can she sing a pretty song?, *etc.*
   She can sing a pretty song,
   But she often sings it wrong, *etc.*

7. How old is she?, *etc.*
   Three times six and four times seven,
   Twenty-eight and eleven!, *etc.*

BY 'N BYE

Thoughtfully (♩ = 72)

Texas

By'n bye, by'n bye. Stars shin-ing, num-ber, num-ber one, num-ber two, num-ber three, Good Lawd, by'n bye, by'n bye, Good Lawd, by'n bye.

Ostinato: tuned instrument

Ostinato: percussion

Chime bars

2. By'n bye, by'n bye.
   Stars shining,
   Number, number four,

   Number five, number six,
   Good Lawd, by'n bye, by'n bye,
   Good Lawd, by'n bye.

The youngest children like to count the stars on their fingers. Lots of other things can be counted, too—birds singing, flowers growing, etc.

From *The American Songbag* by Carl Sandburg, Harcourt Brace Jovanovich, Inc.

THE JACKFISH

Easy-going (♩ = 72)

Virginia

When sung smoothly and with a quiet undulating pulse, this is most effective.

Collected by Cecil Sharp, used by permission of Novello & Co., Ltd., London.

THE RIDDLE SONG
(I GAVE MY LOVE A CHERRY)

Smoothly (♩ = 69)

Kentucky

I gave my love a cher-ry that has no stone, I gave my love a chick-en that has no_ bone, I gave my love a ring_ that has no end, I gave my love a ba-by that's no cry-en.___

Chime bars

2. How can there be a cherry that has no stone?
   How can there be a chicken that has no bone?
   How can there be a ring that has no end?
   How can there be a baby that's no cry-en?

3. A cherry when it's blooming it has no stone,
   A chicken when it's pipping it has no bone,
   A ring when it's rolling it has no end,
   A baby when it's sleeping there's no cry-en.

Collected by Cecil Sharp, used by permission of Novello & Co., Ltd., London.

46

Our friend, Richard Chase, gave us a charming variant that he heard sung in the southern Appalachian Mountains, in place of the "ring" line in each verse:

". . . I told my love a story that has no end,"

". . . How can there be a story that has no end?"

". . . A story when it's telling, it has no end."

YOUNG LAMBS TO SELL

Cheerfully (♩. = 63) *London street song*

Ostinato: tuned instrument

Ostinato: percussion

Chime bars

Originally, this was a street cry for selling little toy lambs made of wool and wood.

* Capo III

THE TOTTENHAM TOAD

With a lilt (♩ = 120)

Virginia

The Tot-ten-ham toad came trot-ting up the road with his feet all swim-ming in the sea. Pret-ty lit-tle squirrel with your tail in curl, they've all got a wife but me. The me.

Ostinato: tuned instrument

Ostinato: percussion

Chime bars

Collected by Cecil Sharp, used by permission of Novello & Co., Ltd., London.

COCK-A-DOODLE-DOO

Gaily (♩ =96)

English tradition

Cock-a- doo-dle- doo! My dame has lost her shoe; my mas-ter's lost his fid-dling stick and doesn't know what to do, and doesn't know what to do, and doesn't know what to do; my mas-ter's lost his fid-dling stick and doesn't know what to do.

Ostinato: tuned instrument

Ostinato: percussion

Chime bars

2. Cock-a-doodle-doo!
   What is my dame to do?
   Till master finds his fiddling stick,
   She'll dance without her shoe.
   She'll dance without her shoe,
   She'll dance without her shoe;
   Till master finds his fiddling stick,
   She'll dance without her shoe.

3. Cock-a-doodle-doo!
   My dame has found her shoe,
   And master's found his fiddling stick,
   Sing doodle-doodle-doo!
   Sing doodle-doodle-doo!
   Sing doodle-doodle-doo!
   And master's found his fiddling stick,
   Sing doodle-doodle-doo!

THE MOCKINGBIRD
(HUSH UP, BABY)

Dreamily (♩ = 90)

North Carolina

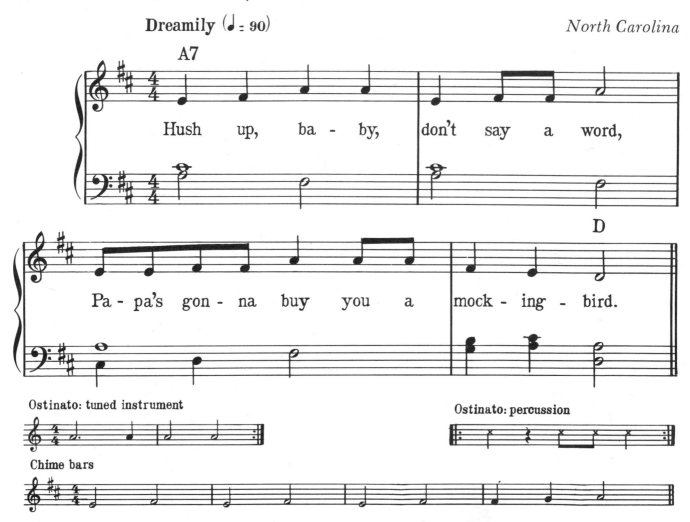

Hush up, ba - by, don't say a word,

Pa - pa's gon - na buy you a mock - ing - bird.

Ostinato: tuned instrument

Chime bars

Ostinato: percussion

2. If it can't whistle, and it can't sing,
   Papa's going to buy you a diamond ring.

3. If that diamond turns to brass,
   Papa's going to buy you a looking glass.

4. If that looking glass gets broke,
   Papa's going to buy you a Billy goat.

5. If that Billy goat runs away,
   Papa's going to buy you another today.

From *English Folk Songs from the Southern Appalachians,* collected by Cecil Sharp, Oxford University Press, London. Used by permission.

DADDY SHOT A BEAR

Enthusiastically (♩ = 88)

Alabama

Dad - dy shot a bear. Dad - dy shot a bear. Shot him through a key - hole and nev - er touched a hair! hair!

Ostinato: tuned instrument

Ostinato: percussion

Chime bars

Children find it irresistible to make up additional verses about Daddy.

THE ALLEE-ALLEE O

Jauntily (♩ = 120)

Rockport, Massachusetts

Oh, the big ship's a-sailing through the Al-lee-al-lee

O, the Al-lee-al-lee O, the Al-lee-al-lee

O! Oh, the big ship's a-sailing through the Al-lee-al-lee

O! Hi! Ding-dong-day!

Ostinato: tuned instrument

Chime bars

Ostinato: percussion

From *Singing Games and Playparty Games* by Richard Chase, Dover Publications, Inc., New York. Reprinted through permission of the publisher.

54

The children of Rockport, Massachusetts, sing this variant as they join hands in a long line and "wind up" around a tree or a stationary figure. This tune must have been brought to our country by early Irish settlers, for it is still popular with the singing children of Ireland.

THE LITTLE PIG

Quietly (♩ = 60)

North Carolina

There _ was an old wo-man who had a lit-tle pig, A-hoo, hoo, hoo. There was an old wo-man who had a lit-tle pig, it did-n't cost much for it was-n't ve-ry big, A-hoo, hoo, hoo.

Ostinato: percussion

Chime bars

2. Oh, that little pig did a heap of harm,
   Ahoo, hoo, hoo.
   It made little tracks all around the barn,
   Ahoo, hoo, hoo.

3. The little old woman fed the pig on clover,
   Ahoo, hoo, hoo.
   And when it died, it died all over,
   Ahoo, hoo, hoo.

Even tiny children can sing this like a sea chantey, joining in on the "Ahoo, hoo, hoo."
This is excellent for matching tones, too.

Collected by Cecil Sharp, used by permission of Novello & Co., Ltd., London.

PHOEBE IN HER PETTICOAT

Simply ($\quarternote$ = 152)

North Carolina

Phoe-be in her pet - ti-coat, Phoe-be in her gown,

Phoe-be in her pet - ti-coat, go-ing down to town.

Ostinato: tuned instrument

Ostinato: percussion

Chime bars

✻ Capo III   Collected by Cecil Sharp, used by permission of Novello & Co., Ltd., London.

LAVENDER'S BLUE

With a gentle swing (♩ = 112)

English tradition

Lav-en-der's blue, did-dle, did-dle, rose-ma-ry's green; when you are
king; did-dle, did-dle, I shall be queen. Who told you so, did-dle, did-dle,
who told you so? 'Twas my own heart, did-dle, did-dle, that told me so.

Ostinato: tuned instrument
Chime bars

Ostinato: percussion

2. Call up your men, diddle, diddle, set them to work,
   Some to the plough, diddle, diddle, some to the cart.
   Some to make hay, diddle, diddle, some to cut corn,
   While you and I, diddle, diddle, keep ourselves warm.

3. If I should die, diddle, diddle, as it may hap,
   I must be buried, diddle diddle, under the tap.
   Who told you so, diddle, diddle, pray tell me why?
   So I may drink, diddle, diddle, when I am dry!

MARY WORE A RED DRESS

Virginia

Ostinato: tuned instrument

Chime bars

Ostinato: percussion

2. Tommy wore a green shirt,
   Green shirt, green shirt,
   Tommy wore a green shirt,
   All day long.

3. Sarah wore a yellow dress,
   Yellow dress, yellow dress,
   Sarah wore a yellow dress,
   All day long.

By singing each other's names, children can quickly learn all the names in a new group, as well as different colors. Sometimes the child likes to choose whether "his verse" should be sung fast or slow, soft or loud, or combinations thereof.

GO AND TELL AUNT NANCY
(OLD GRAY GOOSE)

North Carolina

Quietly (♩= 69)

Go and tell Aunt Nan - cy, go and tell Aunt Nan - cy,

go and tell Aunt Nan - cy the old gray goose is dead.

Ostinato: tuned instrument

Ostinato: percussion

Chime bars

2. The one that she'd been saving,
   The one that she'd been saving,
   The one that she'd been saving
   To make her feather bed.

3. She died last Friday,
   She died last Friday,
   She died last Friday,
   Standing on her head.

4. She left nine little goslings,
   She left nine little goslings,
   She left nine little goslings
   To scratch for their own bread.

Do sing this beautiful tune with a smooth legato!

Collected by Cecil Sharp, used by permission of Novello & Co., Ltd., London.

WILL YOU WEAR RED?

North Carolina

Smoothly (♩=69)

O my love, will you wear red? Will you wear red, Jil-ly Jen-kin? I

won't wear red, for it's the col-or of my head, I'll buy me a dil-low, wear a

dou-ble o-ver dill, I'll buy me a dil-low, wear a dai - sy.

Ostinato: tuned instrument

Ostinato: percussion

Chime bars

2. O my love, will you wear white?
   Will you wear white, Jilly Jenkin?
   I won't wear white, for it's much too light,
   I'll buy me a dillow, wear a double over dill,
   I'll buy me a dillow, wear a daisy.

3. O my love, will you wear green?
   Will you wear green, Jilly Jenkin?
   I won't wear green—it's a shame to be seen,
   I'll buy me a dillow, wear a double over dill,
   I'll buy me a dillow, wear a daisy.

Collected by Cecil Sharp, used by permission of Novello & Co., Ltd., London.

4. O my love, will you wear blue?
   Will you wear blue, Jilly Jenkin?
   I will wear blue—it's the color that is true!
   I'll buy me a dillow, wear a double over dill,
   I'll buy me a dillow, wear a daisy.

Of course, the children will add many colors for Jilly Jenkin to wear, with extravagant rhyme schemes!

FROG WENT A-COURTIN'

Appalachian Mountain tune

✻ Capo III

2. When upon his high horse set, h'm, h'm,
   His boots they shone as black as jet, h'm, h'm.

3. He rode right up to mouse's hall, h'm, h'm,
   Where he most tenderly did call, h'm, h'm:

4. "Oh, Mistress Mouse, are you within?," h'm, h'm.
   "Yes, kind frog, I sit to spin," h'm, h'm.

5. He took Miss Mousie on his knee, h'm, h'm.
   "Pray, Miss Mouse, will you marry me?," h'm, h'm.

6. "Without my Uncle Rat's consent," h'm, h'm,
   "I would not marry the president!," h'm, h'm.

7. Then Uncle Rat he soon comes home, h'm, h'm.
   "Who's been here since I've been gone?," h'm, h'm.

8. "A pretty little dandyman," says she, h'm, h'm.
   "Who swears he wants to marry me," h'm, h'm.

9. "Where will the wedding breakfast be?," h'm, h'm.
   "Way down yonder in a hollow tree," h'm, h'm.

10. "What will the wedding breakfast be?," h'm, h'm.
    "Three green beans and a black-eyed pea," h'm, h'm.

11. "Who will make the wedding gown?," h'm, h'm.
    "Old Miss Rat from Pumpkin Town," h'm, h'm.

12. Then Uncle Rat gave his consent, h'm, h'm.
    And that's the way the marriage went, h'm, h'm.

13. The first to come in was a little white moth, h'm, h'm
    To spread on the tablecloth, h'm, h'm.

14. Next to come in was a big black bug, h'm, h'm.
    On his back was a cider jug, h'm, h'm.

15. Next to come in was Mister Coon, h'm, h'm,
    Waving about a silver spoon, h'm, h'm.

16. Next to come in was a spotted snake, h'm, h'm,
    Passing 'round the wedding cake, h'm, h'm.

17. Next to come in was a bumblebee, h'm, h'm,
    A banjo buckled on his knee, h'm, h'm.

18. Next to come in was a nimble flea, h'm, h'm,
    To dance a jig for the bumblebee, h'm, h'm.

19. Next to come in was the old gray goose, h'm, h'm.
    She picked up her fiddle and she cut loose!, h'm, h'm.

20. Next to come in were two little ants, h'm, h'm,
    Fixin' 'round to have a dance, h'm, h'm.

21. Next to come in was a little ol' fly, h'm, h'm.
    He ate up all the wedding pie, h'm, h'm.

22. Next to come in was a little chick, h'm, h'm.
    He ate so much it made him sick, h'm, h'm.

23. The last to come in was the old tomcat, h'm, h'm.
    He says: "I'll put a stop to that!," h'm, h'm.

24. The frog and the mouse they went to France, h'm, h'm.
    And this is the end of my romance, h'm, h'm.

25. Frog's bridle and saddle are laid on the shelf, h'm, h'm.
    If you want any more, you must sing it yourself!, h'm, h'm.

In a very simple way, children can dance and act out the assemblage of animals
gathering at the wedding. Of added interest and incentive to this particular song
would be the colorful and imaginative picture book illustrated by Feodor Rojankovsky, *Frog Went A-Courtin'*.

WILLIE FOSTER

Lively (♩ = 96)

Northumberland

Willie Foster had a coo,
black and brown about the moo,
open the gate and wish her through,___
Willie Foster's aan coo.

Ostinato: tuned instrument

Chime bars

Ostinato: percussion

2. Willie Foster has a hen,
Cockle butt and cockle ben,
She lays eggs for gentlemen
But none for Willie Foster.

From *A Yacre of Land*, collected by R. Vaughan Williams, Oxford University Press, London. Used by permission.

Singing Games

THERE STANDS A LADY ON A MOUNTAIN

Saucily! (♩=76)

Anglo-American tradition

There stands a lady on a moun-tain, who she is I do not know; all she wants is gold and sil-ver, all she wants is a nice young man. Mad-am, will you walk? Mad-am, will you talk? Mad-am, will you mar-ry me? NO! *(Spoken)*

Not if I buy you a nice arm-chair, to sit in your gar-den while you take the air? NO! There YES!

(Spoken) NO!

(Spoken) YES!

2. There stands a lady on a mountain,
   Who she is I do not know;
   All she wants is gold and silver,
   All she wants is a nice young man.
   Madam, will you walk? Madam, will you talk?
   Madam, will you marry me? NO!

   Not if I buy you a silver spoon,
   To feed your baby in the afternoon? NO!

3. There stands a lady on a mountain,
   Who she is I do not know;
   All she wants is gold and silver,
   All she wants is a nice young man.
   Madam, will you walk? Madam, will you talk?
   Madam, will you marry me? NO!

   Not if I buy you a nice straw hat,
   With seven yards of ribbon a-hanging down your back? YES!

In this acting-out song, the children circle around a "lady" in the center. At "Madam, will you walk?," all stop and question the lady with appropriate pantomiming. She answers them each time most emphatically!

OLD BALD EAGLE

Smoothly (♩ = 104)

Kentucky

Old bald ea-gle sail a-round, day-light is gone.

Old bald ea-gle sail a-round, day-light is gone.

2. Meet Miss Maggie on the floor,
     Daylight is gone.
   Meet Miss Maggie on the floor,
     Daylight is gone.

3. You go ride the old gray mare,
     I'll go ride the roan,
   If you get there before I do,
     Leave my girl alone.

4. Big fine house in Baltimore,
     Sixteen stories high,
   Pretty little girl lives up there,
     Hope she'll never die.

A line of boys faces a line of girls.
1. Partners take hands in a two-handed swing.
2. The lines move forward so that partners meet, then back; twice.
3. The lines face up and follow the top couple as they cast off: boys to the left, girls to the right. The leading couple meets and forms an arch at the bottom.
4. The other couples go under the arch and back to place—ready to repeat the dance with the new top couple.

SALLY GO ROUND THE MOON

Brightly (♩. = 112)

Ireland

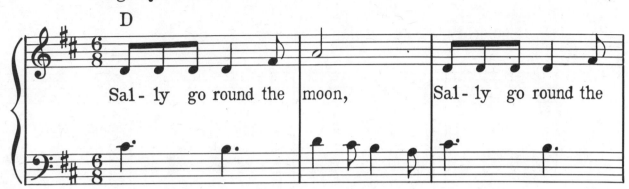

Sal-ly go round the moon,　Sal-ly go round the

stars;　ev-ery Sun-day　af-ter-noon,　WHOOPS! (Shout)

The children join hands and circle to the left at a running walk. On "WHOOPS!" they jump up in place and quickly reverse directions for the repeat, without pausing.

WHEN I WAS A YOUNG GIRL
(OR BOY)

Yorkshire

Smoothly (♩ = 138)

2. When I was a soldier, *etc.*   3. When I was a cowboy, *etc.*   4. When I was a pony, *etc.*

The children join hands and circle around for the first part of each verse. At "Oh, this way and that way," all stop and act out the character.

SANDY LAND

Lightly (♩=176)

Georgia

Make my liv-ing in sand-y land, make my liv-ing in sand-y land, make my liv-ing in sand-y land, la-dies, fare thee well.

2. Raise big 'taters in sandy land,
   Raise big 'taters in sandy land,
   Raise big 'taters in sandy land,
   If you can't dig 'em, I guess I can.

3. Hop, come along, my pretty little miss,
   Hop, come along, my honey,
   Hop, come along, my pretty little miss,
   I won't be home till Sunday.

The children take partners and join hands in a circle.
1. They all take four steps into the center, lifting their hands, and four steps back, dropping hands; then repeat.
2. Each child hooks elbows with his partner and turns around in place.
3. All join hands and skip in a circle.

We have adapted this for the youngest children by circling, hands joined, for verse 1; miming for verse 2; hopping in a circle for verse 3.

From *The Handy Play Party Book*, © 1940 Lynn Rohrbough, Cooperative Recreation Service, Inc., Delaware, Ohio. Used by permission.

OATS AND BEANS

Shropshire

With a good swing (♩.=80)

(1) Oats and beans and bar-ley grow,
(2) First the farm-er sows his seed,

oats and beans and bar-ley grow; do you or I or
then he stands and takes his ease, he stamps his foot and

an-y-one know how oats and beans and bar-ley grow?
claps his hand and turns a-round to view the land.

(3) Wait-ing for a part-ner, wait-ing for a part-ner,

Collected by Cecil Sharp, used by permission of Novello & Co., Ltd., London.

wait-ing for a part-ner, so o-pen the ring and take one in. (4) So

now you're mar-ried, you must o-bey, you must be true to all you say; you

must be wise, you must be good and help your wife to chop the wood.

1. The children join hands and circle to the left around the "farmer" in the center.
2. All stop, facing the center, and act out the words: sowing seed, folding arms at ease, stamping and clapping on the beat, turning around with one hand on brow.
3. The children join hands and swing arms back and forth easily to the music while the farmer chooses a partner.
4. The children skip clockwise while the couple in the center swings.

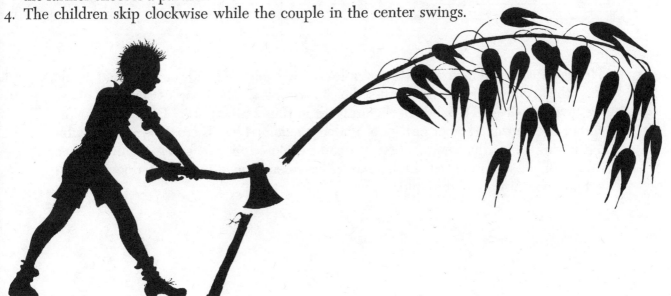

DRAW A BUCKET OF WATER

With a rhythmic swing (♩ = 92)

Sea Island, Georgia

Draw a buck-et of wa - ter for my neigh-bor's daugh - ter. One in a rush— two in a rush— first old man pops un - der.
(lady)

The game is played in groups of four children, two holding hands outstretched, while the other couple joins hands across the first couple's. The couples stand in place, seesawing their joined hands back and forth in time to the music. Each time, at the end of the stanza, a boy or girl "pops under" the joined hands crossed in front, without letting go, so that there is first one child enclosed in the center, then two, then three. Finally, with the last child, a *basket* has been formed by the interlocking arms behind the waists of all the children.

OUR GALLANT SHIP
(THREE TIMES AROUND)

Vigorously (♩ = 72)

Somerset

Three times a-round went our gal-lant ship and three times a-round went she, and three times a-round went our gal-lant ship and we sink to the bot-tom of the sea.

The children join hands in a circle and dance around until the last line, when they suddenly stop and jump slowly four times, once on each beat of the seventh measure. On the word "sea," they sink to the ground—ready to jump up and do it all over again!

Collected by Cecil Sharp, used by permission of Novello & Co., Ltd., London.

GREEN GRAVEL

Shropshire

Gracefully (♩= 138)

Green grav - el, green grav - el, your grass is so green, the fair - est young dam - sel that ev - er was seen. We washed her, we dried her, we clothed her in silk, and we wrote down her

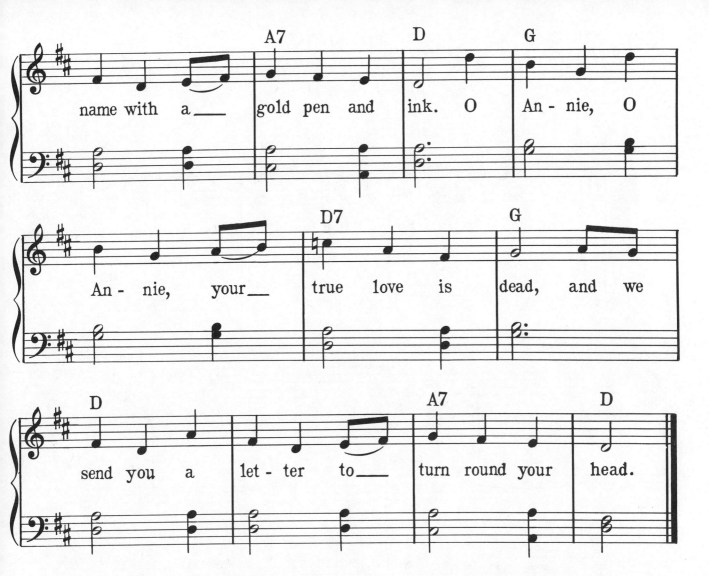

name with a___ gold pen and ink. O An - nie, O

An - nie, your___ true love is dead, and we

send you a let - ter to___ turn round your head.

The children join hands in a ring and walk slowly around, facing inward. As a child's name is sung, she lets go her hands, turns around, and rejoins the ring facing outward. The stanzas are repeated until all names are used and each player has turned round in the ring with his back to the center.

JOLLY IS THE MILLER BOY

With a snappy accent ($\quarternote$ = 132)

Michigan

Jol - ly is the mil - ler boy that lives by the mill;__ the wheel turns round of its own free will. Corn in the hop - per and meal in the sack; the la - dies step for - ward and the gents turn back.

Raining, hailing, cold, stormy weather; in comes the farmer, drinking up his cider. I'll be the reaper, you be the binder; lost my true love, where shall I find her?

Use a small, springy step-hop throughout this singing game. With the girls on their right, boys lead their partners around in a big circle. Extra players are in the center. At "The ladies step forward," girls continue circling in the same direction, while boys reverse direction, single file. Extra players join the single lines. At the very last word, "her," each boy tries to grab a new partner, ready to repeat the game. Leftover players go into the center.

HERE COME TWO DUKES A-RIDING

Jogging along (♩=92)

Kentucky

BOYS:

G — Here come two dukes a - rid - ing, a - rid - ing, a -
D

G — rid - ing, here come two dukes a - rid - ing to my heigh-o ran-som tee.
D7 G

Girls: 2. Oh, what is your good will, sir,
Good will, sir, good will, sir?
Oh, what is your good will, sir?
To my heigh-o ransom tee.

Boys: 3. Our will it is to marry,
To marry, to marry.
Our will it is to marry,
To my heigh-o ransom tee.

Girls: 4. You won't get a one of us, sir,
Of us, sir, of us, sir,
You won't get a one of us, sir,
To my heigh-o ransom tee.

Boys: 5. You're all as stiff as pokers,
As pokers, as pokers,
You're all as stiff as pokers,
To my heigh-o ransom tee.

Girls: 6. We can bend as well as you can,
As you can, as you can,
We can bend as well as you can,
To my heigh-o ransom tee.

Boys: 7. The fairest one that I can see,
That I can see, that I can see,
The fairest one that I can see
Is, come along, Cindy, and go with me!

This is acted back and forth with a line of boys facing a line of girls.

1. The boys march up to greet the girls: forward to half the music, bow, and back into place, miming the high-stepping horses they ride.
2. The girls advance, curtsy, and retire.
3. The boys advance, pretending to doff their big hats as they bow gallantly and retire.
4. The girls turn their backs on the boys and sing haughtily back over their shoulders.
5. The boys step forward stiffly, pointing their fingers in a jeering manner.
6. The girls bend up and down in place.
7. The boys gallop up quickly to the girls, choose a partner, and skip away with her.

OLD ROGER

Somerset

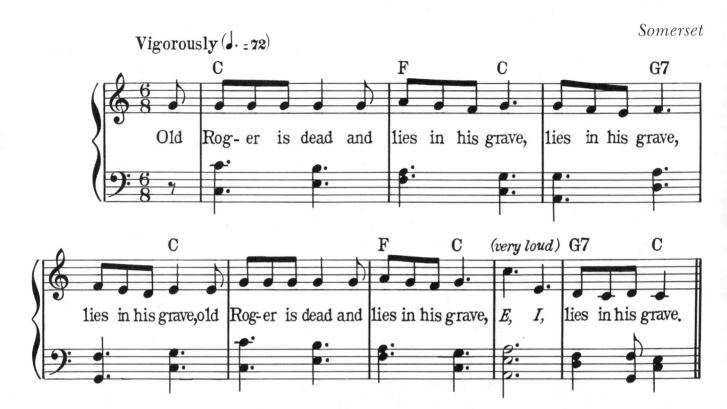

2. They planted an apple tree over his head,
Over his head, over his head,
They planted an apple tree over his head,
E, I, over his head.

3. The apples grew ripe and they all tumbled down, *etc.*

4. There came an old woman a-picking them up, *etc.*

5. Old Roger jumped up and gave her a thump, *etc.*

6. Which made the old woman go hippety hop, *etc.*

Choose three children to represent "Old Roger," "Apple Tree," and "Old Woman."
1. The children join hands and circle around Old Roger, who is lying down in the center.
2. The children stand still, spreading their arms like branches while Apple Tree enters circle and stands at the head of Old Roger.
3. All mime apples falling with their hands.
4. Old Woman enters the circle, picking up apples off the ground.
5. Old Roger leaps up and chases Old Woman inside the circle, pretending to whack her.
6. Old Woman breaks through the circle and hobbles about the outside, back to her original place.

Collected by Cecil Sharp, used by permission of Novello & Co., Ltd., London.

HERE COMES SALLY!

North Carolina

Saucily (♩ = 100)

Here comes Sal-ly down our al-ley, here comes Sal-ly down our al-ley,

here comes Sal-ly down our al-ley, down in North Car-o-li-na!

2. Hands on shoulders, promenade,
Hands on shoulders, promenade,
Hands on shoulders, promenade,
Down in North Carolina!

Couples face each other in a big circle, with boys forming the outside ring and girls the inside ring. Extra girls go into the center as "Sallys." During the first half of the song, Sallys skip clockwise around the inside of the "alley" formed by the couples standing apart and clapping. At the last note of "down in North Caroli-*na*," the Sallys steal partners by skipping up to the nearest boy and placing a hand on his shoulder; then all couples immediately join up and skip together in promenade fashion, "hands on shoulders," around the circle, while new left-out Sallys go into the center to wait for the alley to be formed again.

THE ROMAN SOLDIERS

With determination (♩ = 96)

Bath, England

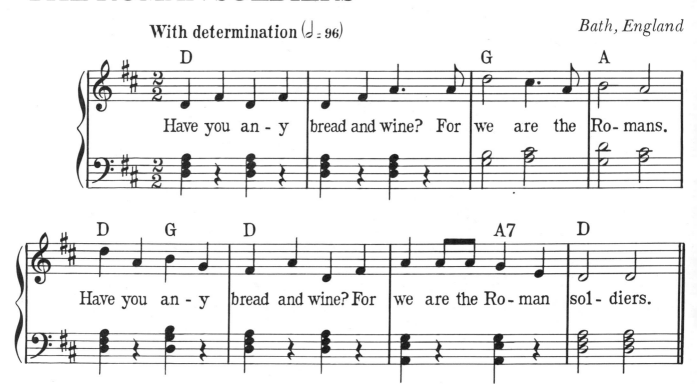

Have you an-y bread and wine? For we are the Ro-mans.

Have you an-y bread and wine? For we are the Ro-man sol-diers.

The children divide into two equal sides—the Romans and the English—and face each other in two lines. They sing alternately, moving four steps forward and backward as they mime the words.

1. Have you any bread and wine?
   For we are the Romans.
   Have you any bread and wine?
   For we are the Roman soldiers.

2. Yes, we have some bread and wine,
   For we are the English.
   Yes, we have some bread and wine,
   For we are the English soldiers.

3. Then we will have one cupful,
   For we are the Romans, *etc.*

4. No, you shan't have one cupful,
   For we are the English, *etc.*

5. We will tell the King on you,
   For we are the Romans, *etc.*

6. We don't care for the King or you,
   For we are the English, *etc.*

7. We will send our cats to scratch,
   For we are the Romans, *etc.*

8. We don't care for your cats or you,
   For we are the English, *etc.*

9. We will send our dogs to bite,
   For we are the Romans, *etc.*

10. We don't care for your dogs or you,
    For we are the English, *etc.*

11. Are you ready for a fight?
    For we are the Romans, *etc.*

12. Yes, we're ready for a fight,
    For we are the English, *etc.*

Both sides stand still and shout, "SHOOT, BANG, FIRE!" then all form a circle and walk around, acting and singing the following verses:

13. Now we've only got one arm,
    For we are the Romans,
                English,
    Now we've only got one arm,
    For we are the Roman soldiers.
                English soldiers.

14. Now we've only got one leg, *etc.*

15. Now we've only got one eye, *etc.*

16. Now we all are dead and gone, *etc.* (Children lie down on the floor.)

17. Then we'll skip in a merry ring, *etc.* (Children jump up and skip in a circle.)

THE NOBLE DUKE OF YORK

Steadily (♩=100)

Derbyshire

(1.) Oh, the no-ble Duke of York, he had ten thou-sand men; he marched them up to the top of the hill and he marched them down a - gain.

(2.) Now ___ when they were up, they were up; and when they were down, they were down; and when they were on - ly ___ half - way up, they were nei - ther up nor down.

With the same beat

(3.) Oh! A-hunt-ing we will go, ___ a-hunt-ing we will go; ___ we'll catch a fox and put him in a box, and then we'll let him go.

Two lines of children face one another.
1. The top couple takes hands and marches down between the lines, turning on the word "men" and marching back to place.
2. The top couple skips around the outside, down to the bottom place, and forms an arch.
3. All the other couples join hands and skip around to the bottom, through the arch, and back to place (the verse being repeated as often as necessary).

The game is repeated with the new head couple.

TWO IN A BOAT

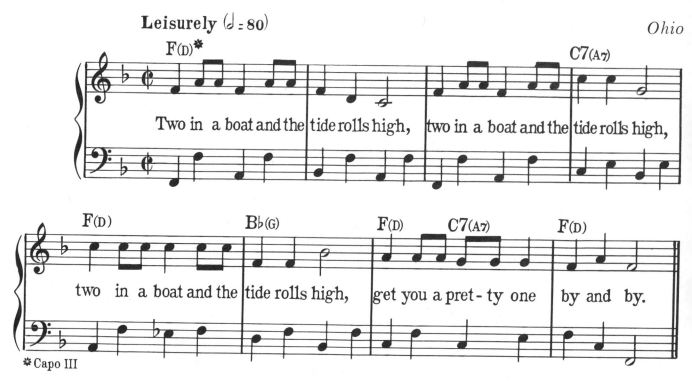

Leisurely (♩=80)

F(D)✻ ... C7(A7)

Two in a boat and the tide rolls high, two in a boat and the tide rolls high,

F(D) ... Bb(G) ... F(D) ... C7(A7) ... F(D)

two in a boat and the tide rolls high, get you a pret-ty one by and by.

✻ Capo III

2. Four in a boat and the tide rolls high,
Four in a boat and the tide rolls high,
Four in a boat and the tide rolls high,
Get you a pretty one by-and-by.

3. Eight in a boat and it won't go round,
Eight in a boat and it won't go round,
Eight in a boat and it won't go round,
Swing that pretty one you've just found.

The children join hands and circle to the left around two boys in the center, who circle inside in the opposite direction. At the words "Get you a pretty one," the two boys each choose a partner. The game is repeated with all four center children choosing partners. At "Swing that pretty one," the four couples swing two hands around. Then all join the outside ring, and the game is repeated with two girls in the center.

Younger children enjoy acting out the song freely on the floor and substituting verses, such as, "Rowing in the boat," "Paddling in the boat," "Bailing out the boat."

From *The Handy Play Party Book,* © 1940 Lynn Rohrbough, Cooperative Recreation Service, Inc., Delaware, Ohio. Used by permission.

BOW DOWN, O BELINDA

Virginia

Brightly (♩ = 104)

Bow down, O Be-lin-da, bow down, O Be-lin-da, bow down, O Be-lin-da, won't you be my part-ner?

2. Into the middle, O Belinda,
    Out of the middle, O Belinda,
  Into the middle, O Belinda,
    Won't you be my partner?

3. Skip in a circle, O Belinda,
    Skip in a circle, O Belinda,
  Skip in a circle, O Belinda,
    Won't you be my partner?

4. Both hands round, O Belinda,
    Both hands round, O Belinda,
  Both hands round, O Belinda,
    Won't you be my partner?

We have revised the traditional longways movements so as to be suitable for young children.

Verse 1: The children form a circle and "bow" slowly to each other three times.
Verse 2: All join hands and take four steps into the middle and four out; four in, four out.
Verse 3: Children choose any partner for a two-handed swing.

Children often devise other verses: "Clap your hands, O Belinda," or
                                     "Swing your arms, O Belinda," or
                                     "Hop up and down, O Belinda," etc.

FLOATING DOWN THE RIVER
(JUMP JOSIE)

Smoothly (♩.=64)

Tennessee

We're float - ing down the riv - er, we're float - ing down be - low; we're float - ing down the riv - er to the O - hi - o.

Twice as fast! (♩=108)

Two in the mid - dle and you can't jump Jo - sie,

✿ Capo III

two in the mid-dle and you can't jump Jo-sie,

two in the mid-dle and you can't jump Jo-sie,

oh, my Su-san Brown. _____

2. We're floating down the river, *etc.*
Four in the middle and you can't jump Josie, *etc.*

3. We're floating down the river, *etc.*
Eight in the middle and you can't jump Josie, *etc.*

4. We're floating down the river, *etc.*
Get out of there if you can't jump Josie, *etc.*

The children join hands and circle slowly to the left around one child, who chooses a partner from the ring. At "Two in the middle," the ring stands still and claps in rhythm while the children in the center jump up and down or skip around on the spot in a two-handed swing. The sequence is then repeated, from "floating down the river," with new partners chosen, until verse four, when the eight children scamper out of the center and join the ring.

CAPTAIN JINKS

American square dance

Briskly (♩.=104)

When__ Cap - tain Jinks comes home at night, he

claps his hands with all his might. Sa - lute your part - ner,

smile so bright, for that's the style in the ar - my.

Join your hands and for - ward all,

Da Capo al Fine

back-ward all, back-ward all; join your hands and

for - ward all, for that's the style in the ar - my.

2. When Captain Jinks comes home at night,
      The gentleman passes to the right.
   Swing your partner so polite,
      For that's the style in the army.
   Promenade around the hall,
      Around the hall, around the hall;
   Promenade around the hall,
      For that's the style in the army.

Just suit the actions to the words in this circle dance. We usually use only the first verse for the younger children.

Older children may prefer to dance this with partners, so that in the second verse the boy can cross in front of his partner at "The gentleman passes to the right," and take the partner of the boy on his right to "Promenade around the hall."

GOING TO BOSTON

Jauntily (♩=100)

Kentucky

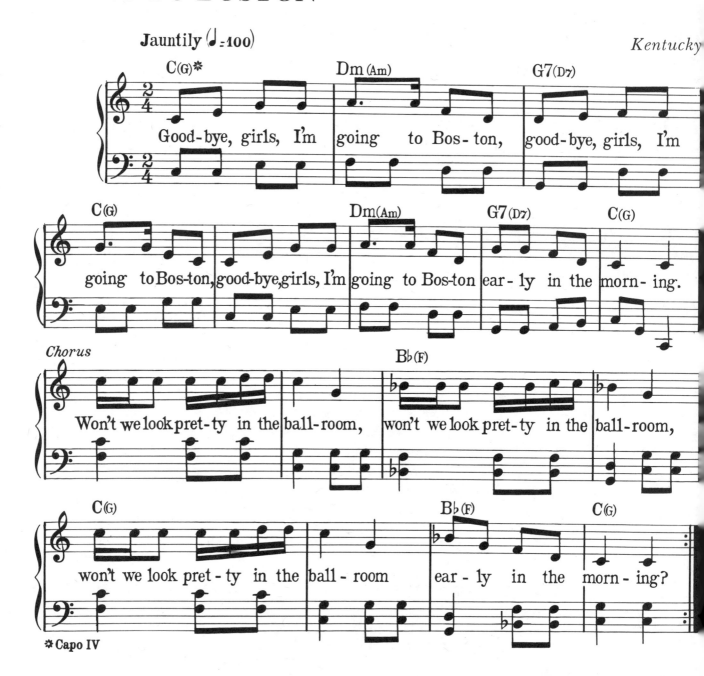

Good-bye, girls, I'm going to Bos-ton, good-bye, girls, I'm going to Bos-ton, good-bye, girls, I'm going to Bos-ton ear-ly in the morn-ing.

Chorus

Won't we look pret-ty in the ball-room, won't we look pret-ty in the ball-room, won't we look pret-ty in the ball-room ear-ly in the morn-ing?

✲ Capo IV

2. Saddle up, boys, and let's go with them,
Saddle up, boys, and let's go with them,
Saddle up, boys, and let's go with them,
Early in the morning.
CHORUS

3. Swing your partner all the way to Boston,
Swing your partner all the way to Boston,
Swing your partner all the way to Boston,
Early in the morning.
CHORUS

A line of boys faces a line of girls.

1. The line of girls skips, following the leader, around the boys, coming back in time for the chorus, which all clap and sing in place for each verse.
2. The line of boys gallops around the girls and back to place for the chorus.
3. The girls and boys opposite each other take hands and skip gently in a two-handed swing, again lining up in time to sing and clap the chorus.

Action Songs

HERE WE COME ON OUR PONIES

Flemish folk tune
WORDS BY RICHARD COMPTON

Galloping along (♩.= 112)

One group can sing the words while a second group acts them out: galloping on their ponies; reining them in; bowing how-do-you-do to each other; then galloping off again.

From *140 Folk Songs*, Concord Series #7, © E. C. Schirmer Music Company, Boston, Mass. Used by permission.

THE BIG PROCESSION

SATIS COLEMAN
ALICE THORN

Children love to substitute their own names in this marching song. We use it in a multitude of ways: "marching out to play," "marching in to rest," etc. It is also an excellent song for introducing percussion instruments, and we sometimes have a whole "band" marching around the room!

From *Singing Time* by Satis N. Coleman and Alice G. Thorn. Copyright © 1929 by Satis N. Coleman and Alice G. Thorn. Used by permission of The John Day Company, Inc., publisher.

THIS OLD MAN

Steadily (♩ = 152)

English tradition

2. This old man, he played two,
   He played nicknack on my shoe,
   Nicknack paddywhack, give a dog a bone,
   This old man came rolling home.

3. This old man, he played three,
   He played nicknack on my knee,
   Nicknack paddywhack, give a dog a bone,
   This old man came rolling home.

4. This old man, he played four,
   He played nicknack on the floor,
   Nicknack paddywhack, give a dog a bone,
   This old man came rolling home.

The children can sit on the floor and mime the actions as they sing: holding one finger up; tapping the other thumb with it; pretending to give a dog a bone; revolving one arm around the other for "rolling home." Children will naturally sway in rhythm, and new verses will be made up on the spot.

HOT CROSS BUNS

Firmly (♩ = 76)

English tradition

Hot cross buns! Hot cross buns!

One a pen - ny, two a pen - ny, hot cross buns!

Fun for rhythmic walking, clapping, or percussion. The children can easily work out the different beats of this song.

PICK A BALE OF COTTON

Texas

(Back to sign 𝄋 for additional verses)

2. Me and my brother can pick a bale of cotton,
Me and my brother can pick a bale a day.
Oh, lawdy, pick a bale of cotton,
Oh, lawdy, pick a bale a day.

3. Went to Mississippi to pick a bale of cotton,
Went to Mississippi to pick a bale a day.
Oh, lawdy, pick a bale of cotton,
Oh, lawdy, pick a bale a day.

4. Pick-a, pick-a, pick-a, pick-a, pick-a bale of cotton,
Pick-a, pick-a, pick-a, pick-a, pick-a bale a day.
Oh, lawdy, pick a bale of cotton,
Oh, lawdy, pick a bale a day.

SEE HOW I'M JUMPING

Briskly (♩=80)

Flemish folk tune

See how I'm jump-ing, jump-ing, jump-ing! See how I'm bounc-ing like a ball! You did-n't know I could jump so high; you did-n't know I could stand so still. See how I'm jump-ing, jump-ing, jump-ing! When I am tired, down I flop.

After the children learn the words, they love to act this out, jumping lightly in time to the music and staying absolutely motionless on "stand so still" for a long pause. At the end they flop down on the floor.

From *First Solo Book* by Angela Diller and Elizabeth Quaile. Copyright 1928 by G. Schirmer, Inc. Used by permission.

JIM ALONG, JOSIE

Gaily (♩=92)

The Ozark Mountains

F(D)✱

Hey,　jim a - long,　jim a - long, Jo - sie;

B♭(G)

F(D)

hey,　jim a - long,

C7(A7)　　F(D)

jim a - long, Joe.

✱ Capo III

2. Hop, jim along, jim along, Josie,
   Hop, jim along, jim along, Joe.

3. Jump, jim along, jim along, Josie,
   Jump, jim along, jim along, Joe.

4. Fly, jim along, jim along, Josie,
   Fly, jim along, jim along, Joe.

5. Skip, jim along, jim along, Josie,
   Skip, jim along, jim along, Joe.

Variant of song collected by B. A. Botkin. From *The American Play-Party Song*, published by the University of Nebraska Press. Copyright © 1937, 1963 by B. A. Botkin. Reprinted by permission of Curtis Brown, Ltd.

POLLY PERKIN

Precisely ($\quad$=84)

The Netherlands

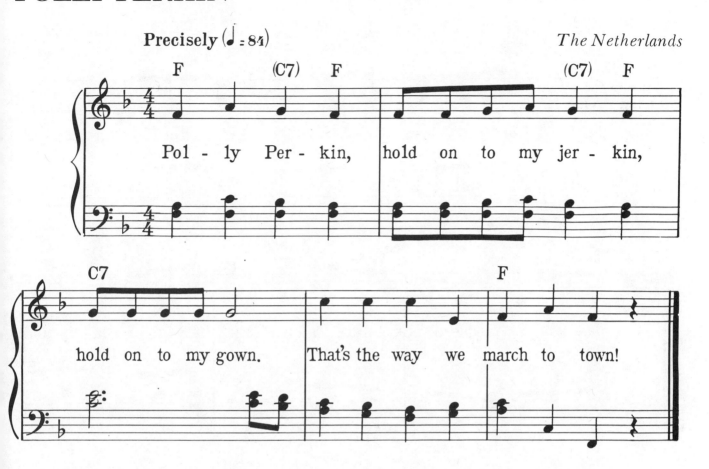

Pol - ly Per - kin, hold on to my jer - kin,

hold on to my gown. That's the way we march to town!

The youngest children love to march to this in a long line, holding onto the shirt or dress of the child in front.

HUSH-A-BYE, BABY

Smoothly rocking (♩. = 44)

ANGELA DILLER

Hush-a-bye, ba-by, thy cra-dle is green; fa-ther's a no-ble-man, moth-er's a queen; and Bet-ty's a la-dy and wears a gold ring; and John-ny's a drum-mer and drums for the king!

Children can mime the rocking cradle and the characters and beat an imaginary drum in time for "drúms fór thé kíng."

From *A Pre-School Music Book* by Angela Diller and Kate Stearns Page. Copyright 1936 by G. Schirmer, Inc. Used by permission.

CREEP, MOUSE, CREEP

Stealthily (♩=69)

ANGELA DILLER

Creep, mouse, creep! The old cat lies a-sleep; the dog's a-way, the kit-tens play; creep, mouse, creep!

❀ Capo III

The "old cat" pretends to sleep on the floor. The other children, as mice, tiptoe silently around the cat, in time to the music. Sometimes the cat wakes up at the very end, and the mice scamper for safety!

From *A Pre-School Music Book* by Angela Diller and Kate Stearns Page.
Copyright 1936 by G. Schirmer, Inc. Used by permission.

111

JOHN BROWN HAD A LITTLE INDIAN

Lightly (♩= 92)   *American tradition*

John Brown had a lit - tle In - dian,
John Brown had a lit - tle In - dian, John Brown
had a lit - tle In - dian, one lit - tle In - dian boy.

2. One little, two little, three little Indians,
   Four little, five little, six little Indians,
   Seven little, eight little, nine little Indians,
   Ten little Indian boys.

3. Ten little, nine little, eight little Indians,
   Seven little, six little, five little Indians,
   Four little, three little, two little Indians,
   One little Indian boy!

This can be used for finger play. The faster you sing it, the trickier it is!

PUNCHINELLO

Saucily (♩ = 108)

American tradition

C

What can you do, Pun-chi-nel-lo, fun-ny fel - low?

G7 **C**

What can you do, Pun-chi-nel-lo, fun-ny you?

2. We can do it too, Punchinello, funny fellow!
   We can do it too, Punchinello, funny you!

3. You choose one of us, Punchinello, funny fellow!
   You choose one of us, Punchinello, funny you!

This is a circle game with children taking turns in the center, making up motions for the others to copy.

SING A SONG OF SIXPENCE

Lyrically (♩=92)   *English tradition*

Sing a song of six-pence, a pock-et-ful of rye;
four and twen-ty black-birds baked in a pie! When the pie was o-pened, the
birds be-gan to sing; was-n't that a dain-ty dish to set be-fore the king?

2. The king was in his counting house,
   Counting out his money.
   The queen was in the parlor,
   Eating bread and honey.
   The maid was in the garden,
   Hanging out the clothes,
   When down came a blackbird
   And snipped off her nose!

This can be mimed individually or played as a circle game, walking around until "four and twenty," when the children stop and stretch their arms toward the center as the "pie." At the words, "When the pie was opened," they can raise their arms high and then flap them for birds. In the second verse, the children mime the actions of each character.

114

POP! GOES THE WEASEL

Sprightly (♩.= 92)

Square dance tune from Iowa

All a-round the cob - bler's bench, the mon-key chased the wea - sel; the mon-key thought 'twas all in fun. Pop! goes the wea - sel. A pen - ny for a spool of thread, a nick - el for a nee - dle; that's the way the mon-ey goes. Pop! goes the wea-sel.

We often play this as a circle game, walking or skipping around during the first part, and jumping or clapping on "Pop," then swinging our joined hands for "A penny for a spool of thread."

THE NORTH WIND DOTH BLOW

Smoothly (♩. = 44)   *English tradition*

2. The north wind doth blow,
   And we shall have snow,
   And what will the dormouse do then, poor thing?
   Rolled up like a ball,
   In his nest, snug and small,
   He'll sleep till warm weather comes in, poor thing!

Children can mime the wind and snow with their arms, then huddle down, with their heads under their arms, for the robin.

HICKORY, DICKORY, DOCK

Briskly (♩. = 63)

English tradition

Children like to clap or use percussion on the "ticktocks" and on the clock striking "one," as well as to mime the mouse running up and down the clock with their fingers.

117

A-HUNTING WE WILL GO

Jogging along (♩ = 92)

England

Oh! A- hunt-ing we will go, a-hunt-ing we will go; we'll catch a fox and put him in a box and then we'll let him go.

This is a great favorite of the younger children to act out and to make up additional verses about other animals: "We'll catch a bear and put him in a chair," etc.

JEREMIAH, BLOW THE FIRE

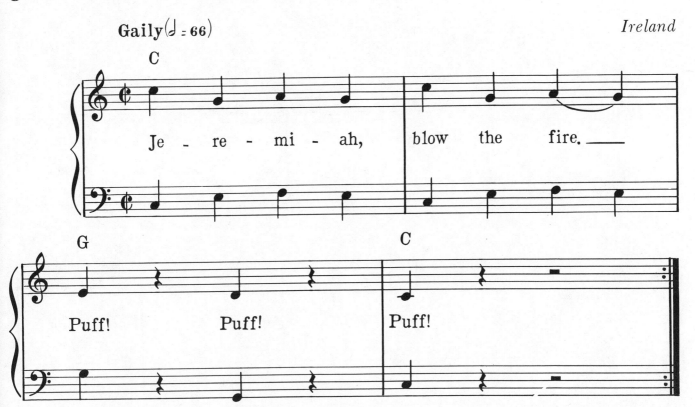

Gaily (♩ = 66)   *Ireland*

Je - re - mi - ah,   blow   the   fire. ___

Puff!   Puff!   Puff!

The children join hands and walk in a ring, then stop, facing the center, and jump
on the "puffs": once in place, once into the middle, once out again—then circle in
the opposite direction!

LITTLE BETTY MARTIN

Lightly (♩ = 160)

Virginia

Lit - tle Bet - ty Mar - tin, tip - py toe, tip - py toe;

lit - tle Bet - ty Mar - tin, tip - toe fine. She

could - n't find a hus - band to suit her, to suit her, she

could - n't find a hus - band to suit her fine.

A song for tiptoeing. The children can either sing or tiptoe, or both at the same time.

LONDON HILL

English tradition

Brightly (♩ = 152)

As I went o - ver Lon - don Hill,
Lon - don Hill, Lon - don Hill, as I went o - ver
Lon - don Hill on a cold, fros - ty morn - ing.

2. I shook my foot on London Hill,
London Hill, London Hill,
I shook my foot on London Hill
On a cold, frosty morning.

3. I shook my head on London Hill,
London Hill, London Hill,
I shook my head on London Hill
On a cold, frosty morning.

Let the actions suit the words and encourage the children to make up their own verses: "I jumped like a frog on London Hill"; "I drove my car on London Hill."

SANTY MALONEY

Irish tradition

Here we go, Santy Maloney,
here we go, Santy Maloney,
here we go, Santy Maloney,
as we go round and round!

2. Tap — your hand on your shoulder,
Tap — your hand on your shoulder,
Tap — your hand on your shoulder,
As we go round and round.

3. Here we go, Santy Maloney,
Here we go, Santy Maloney,
Here we go, Santy Maloney,
As we go round and round.

4. Tap — your hand on your knee — ,
Tap — your hand on your knee — ,
Tap — your hand on your knee — ,
As we go round and round.

The children join hands and circle at a skip or running walk. For the second verse, they stand still and tap their shoulders in time to the music. This game can go on for as long as the children make up verses!

SEE-SAW, SACRA-DOWN

Rocking (♩. = 56)

English

See - saw, Sac - ra - down, which is the way to Lon - don town? One foot up and one foot down, this is the way to Lon - don town.

The children stand with one foot in front of the other and rock back and forth with their arms stretched out sideways.

Index of Titles

A-Hunting We Will Go, 118
Allee-Allee O, The, 54
All the Ducks, 25
Ally Bally, 35

Big Procession, The, 103
Billy Boy, 42
Bobby Shaftoe, 34
Bow Down, O Belinda, 93
Brother Rabbit, 28
By'n Bye, 44

Captain Jinks, 96
Cock-a-Doodle-Doo, 50
Cocky Robin, 32
Creep, Mouse, Creep, 111

Daddy Shot a Bear, 53
Draw a Bucket of Water, 78

Floating Down the River, 94
Frog Went A-Courtin', 64

Go and Tell Aunt Nancy, 61
God, Our Loving Father, 31
Going to Boston, 98
Good-bye, Old Paint, 14
Green Gravel, 80

Here Comes Sally!, 87
Here Come Two Dukes A-Riding, 84
Here We Come on Our Ponies, 102
Hickory, Dickory, Dock, 117
Hoosen Johnny, 36
Hop Up, My Ladies, 18
Hot Cross Buns, 105

Hush-a-bye, Baby, 110
Hush Up, Baby, 52

If All the World Were Paper, 26
I Gave My Love a Cherry, 46
I Had a Little Nut Tree, 41

Jackfish, The, 45
Jeremiah, Blow the Fire, 119
Jim Along, Josie, 108
John Brown Had a Little Indian, 112
Johnny, Get Your Hair Cut, 15
Jolly Is the Miller Boy, 82
Jump Josie, 94

Keel Row, The, 16

Lavender's Blue, 58
Lazy John, 38
Little Betty Martin, 120
Little Black Bull, The, 36
Little Pig, The, 56
London Hill, 122

Mary Wore a Red Dress, 60
Mockingbird, The, 52
Muffin Man, The, 27

Noble Duke of York, The, 90
North Wind Doth Blow, The, 116

Oats and Beans, 76
Oh, Dear! What Can the Matter Be?, 22
Old Bald Eagle, 72
Old Gray Goose, 61

Old Roger, 86
Our Gallant Ship, 79

Phoebe in Her Petticoat, 57
Pick a Bale of Cotton, 106
Polly Perkin, 109
Polly, Put the Kettle On, 40
Pop! Goes the Weasel, 115
Punchinello, 113

Riddle Song, The, 46
Roman Soldiers, The, 88

Sally Go Round the Moon, 73
Sandy Land, 75
Santy Maloney, 123
See How I'm Jumping, 107
See-saw, Sacra-down, 124
Shanghai Chicken, 21
Sing a Song of Sixpence, 114

There Stands a Lady on a Mountain, 70
This Little Light o' Mine, 20
This Old Man, 104
Three Times Around, 79
To People Who Have Gardens, 30
Tottenham Toad, The, 49
Two in a Boat, 92

When I was a Young Girl (or Boy), 74
Who Built the Ark?, 24
Willie Foster, 67
Will You Wear Red?, 62

Young Lambs to Sell, 48